LEADER'S
EDITION

Where Do You Think Sex Came From?

RICHARD ▼ DUNN

Student books
are available for use
in group study

VICTOR BOOKS®

A DIVISION OF SCRIPTURE PRESS PUBLICATIONS INC.
USA CANADA ENGLAND

ABOUT THE AUTHOR

RICHARD DUNN is Chairman of the Youth Ministry Department at Trinity College in Deerfield, Illinois. He has over 10 years' experience in youth ministry, and is a popular retreat and conference speaker as well as a Youth Ministry Consultant for Lay Renewal Ministries of St. Louis, Missouri. Small group ministry is a primary focus as he disciples students and equips them for leadership.

All Bible quotations, unless otherwise indicated, are from the *Holy Bible, New International Version,* © 1973, 1978, 1984, International Bible Society. Used by permission of Zondervan Bible Publishers.

ISBN: 0-89693-194-3

1 2 3 4 5 6 7 8 9 10 Printing/Year 95 94 93 92 91

CONTENTS

INTRODUCTION

Small Group Studies

Small group studies are designed to create an environment for your group members which will (1) provide acceptance for them just as they are, (2) challenge them with God's truth to be who He calls them to be, and (3) offer a supportive community to strengthen their personal and spiritual growth. Within the context of meaningful, interpersonal relationships, each session seeks the healing and wholeness of persons through their personal encounters with the grace and holiness of Jesus Christ. Just as the community grew together in Acts 2, as the body served together in 1 Corinthians 12, and the church was equipped together in Ephesians 4, so will your group experience the reality that in Christ we become more than just the sum of our individual members when we meet together, just as we are, to become just who He calls us to be.

Contemporary culture, specifically that of adolescents, offers very little opportunity for interpersonal intimacy. Students need a safe place for healing and a supportive place for growth into wholeness. They need a place to go where they can take off the masks they use to cover insecurity and uncertainty about who they are as persons. They are also searching for a place where they can find meaning through making a contribution to the lives of others. Your students require the security of belonging to a significant community of peers in order to develop their own identity in Christ. Small group studies enable you to meet these needs for individuals who are at all levels of personal and spiritual maturity. The only prerequisite for being a member of these small groups is a heart willing to develop relationships with friends. The potential for growth is as limitless as the potential for God's work in your individual and corporate lives.

To introduce you to the process of small group studies, an overview of the format has been provided.

SESSION OVERVIEW
Each session begins with a summary of the small group experience which has been prepared for your group.

Purpose states the intent of the session, clearly defining the overall thrust of this particular small group experience.

Needs briefly examines the needs of group members in relation to the topic and Scripture. Attention is given to the interpersonal structure of each session.

Goals list objectives by which you can (1) adapt the materials specifically for the context of the small group with which you are working and (2) evaluate the effectiveness of the session in measurable terms.

Life Response suggests a commitment each group member can make in living out the lesson during the week. Additional suggestions for groups with higher commitment levels follow each session.

Resource Materials outlines what you will need in order to lead the group through the process of each session.

HEARTBEAT

These opening exercises and experiences are designed to take a pulse, to get to the heart of who students are. They focus group members on the question, "Who am I?" Active listening and accurate affirmation are the key ingredients in this first step toward community building.

 ## LIFELINE

Discovery is the dynamic element in these active studies of God's Word. The personal, practical exploration of "who I am called to be" is the focus of the group's interaction with biblical truth. As group members deepen in their knowledge and broaden in their understanding of Jesus Christ's lordship, they will be directed toward relevant application of this truth in their own personal context.

 ## BODYLIFE

Your group members will experience the reality of the love of the Body as they commit themselves corporately to being all of who God calls them to be. Personal ownership of the truth discovered in LIFELINE enables students to make new commitments toward personal and spiritual growth. Through affirmation, prayer, and encouragement, they will realize that the love in Christian peer support is greater than the fear of the world's peer pressure.

HINTS & HELPS

☞ **HELPS:** are provided to sensitize you to student concerns and questions which may arise in response to the topic or structure of the session. These insights and resources will help you prepare for the challenges of leading a small group through the community experience of being who God calls them to be.

☞ **HINTS:** are provided to develop your own small group leadership skills. These technical points of advice will support you in your challenging role.

GROUP MEMBER AND LEADER MATERIALS

Group members' workbooks include the main content of the HEARTBEAT, LIFELINE, and BODYLIFE sections of each session. All of the group members' material is reproduced in your leader's edition. Additional exercises and activities in the leader's edition are printed in **boldface**. These additional resources are designed to allow you maximum flexibility for working with your group.

PREPARATION

Your preparation as leader will consist mainly of becoming familiar with the purposes, needs, and goals of each session and adapting the session content in light of your own group. Some groups will need to begin the series with an added emphasis upon the HEARTBEAT section. Other groups, either because of group members' personal maturity or depth of relationships, will have a community foundation which will enable them to focus more time in the LIFELINE and BODYLIFE sections. In either case, you will be prepared to meet students at their points of need.

Group members will not need to prepare in advance for the sessions. As the LIFELINE and BODYLIFE sections become more of a reality, however, student commitments will establish the need for follow-through and loving, community accountability. This accountability can be very naturally incorporated into the following session's HEARTBEAT section once students have progressed to this point.

Prayer will be the ultimate source of preparation for both you and your group. The materials provided for you will encourage and support your efforts to integrate prayer into every phase of this small group series.

▼

Just Say Yes!

SESSION OVERVIEW

Purpose:

"Just Say Yes!" begins a six-week series designed to enable your group members to understand who God created them to be sexually and how they can express that in a way which glorifies Him. Group members will discover that the command "Don't have sex until you are married" has a corollary positive message: "Be the person I created you to be by expressing your sexuality according to My will." This first time together will focus group members' attention on God's view of sex and sexuality.

Needs:

Developmentally, adolescents are beginning to come to terms with sexually maturing bodies. As their bodies and hormones are enduring traumatic physical changes, their thoughts and feelings are also expanding, moving rapidly toward adulthood.

Unfortunately, they are a part of a culture which emphasizes the fulfillment of their physical desires. As a result contemporary adolescents often confuse *sensuality* with *sex-*

uality. Sex outside of the intimacy of marital fulfillment can satisfy immediate sensual and emotional wants, but only God's design can truly fulfill lasting sexual needs.

Adolescents need to develop a wholistic view of sexuality that incorporates God's view of what it means to be male or female and how that can be expressed in the way God intended, for His glory.

Goals:

The *leader's* goals include
(1) affirming group members' positive sexual identity as the male or female God created each of them to be;
(2) enabling group members to identify lust and how it can be resisted;
(3) creating an atmosphere in which group members are comfortable to share their thoughts and feelings about their own sexuality.

The *group members'* goals are
(1) differentiating between sexuality and sensuality;
(2) accurately evaluating their own sexuality from God's point of view;
(3) learning to submit to God's will for their expression of personal sexuality.

Life Response:

Group members will complete the following statements based on their understanding of God's point of view presented in the LIFELINE section:
  a. Sexuality is. . . .
  b. Sensuality is. . . .

Resource Materials:

___ copies of *Where Do You Think Sex Came From?*
___ pens
___ Bibles

HEARTBEAT

INTRODUCTORY ACTIVITY: Group members will draw numbers out of a hat on each turn. The numbers will correspond to a list such as the following:

1. weekend activity
2. school teacher
3. food
4. school subject
5. movie or television show
6. book or magazine
7. place to go for vacation
8. career
9. pizza topping

Begin with the group members telling their favorite items in the category which corresponds to the number which has been drawn. Then go to the second round where members will identify their least favorite or undesirable items they can think of in the specific category.

If the group has a lot of members who are unfamiliar with each other, the above activity will encourage students to talk to one another and not just be in the group. It also will prepare them for their first discovery learning activity in this group experience.

If the group is strong in its relational bonds, the "warm-up" interaction may also assist you in representing this group as a place for members to come and be themselves. You may, however, want to add depth to this activity by using a list such as the following:

1. quality in a friend
2. way to spend time with my family
3. Christmas season activity
4. personal characteristic or quality
5. being known to others as a Christian
6. small group discussion

7. people in my school
8. parent's or guardian's relationship to me
9. thought about my future

Another option for a group which is already comfortable together is to have members share why they came to the group and what their prayers would be—both on a personal and group level—during the next six meetings.

☞ [HINT: Whatever method you use to introduce group members, get them involved in the discussion and be sure to affirm each contribution by the members as significant and appreciated.]

☞ [HINT: Small groups should always begin with everyone seated comfortably in a circle. Each person should be able to make eye contact with every other person in the group.]

Surveying Attitudes About Sex

Opinion polls. You find them in magazines and newspapers as well as on a variety of television programs. Politics, religion, legal issues, and moral issues are among the hottest topics of opinion polls. Fifty-four percent of the people believe this leader should resign, 39% of the people want to change a law, or 76% of the people accept a certain act as immoral are the type of statistics which reflect public opinion.

To begin the *Where Do You Think Sex Came From?* series together, we begin a simulation of public opinion on another "hot topic": SEX.

Sexual Values Survey

Which of the following statements best reflects your idea of what level of relationship is required for sexual intercourse to be acceptable?

1. Sex with someone you are married to is acceptable.

2. Sex with someone you are engaged to is acceptable.

3. Sex with someone you are seriously dating is acceptable.

4. Sex with someone you have known and care about is acceptable.

5. Sex with someone you really like is acceptable.

6. Sex with someone you have known casually is acceptable.

7. Sex with someone you have just met is acceptable.

To simulate this opinion poll, choose the statements from the above list which you think each of the following individuals or groups would choose if they were answering the survey. Write the number of that statement in the blank.

_____ Your parents or guardians

_____ Your pastor

_____ The majority of the students at your school

_____ Pornographic magazine editors

_____ Peers you know to be sexually active

_____ Hollywood movie directors

_____ Most secular musicians

_____ God

☞ **[HINT: After group members complete their answers, discuss with the group how they responded and how they feel about these opinions. Then use the next question to discover their perception of the sexual values in their immediate sphere of influence, their peers at school.]**

Consider what would happen if you asked all of the students in your school to respond to this survey. In front of each statement, write "M" if you think most students would agree with the statement, "S" if you think several would agree, and "F" if you think only a few would agree.

You will receive all types of messages and opinions about sex, from the media to your school to your home to your church. It can be very confusing if some of those around you are saying, "Go ahead, have sex!" while others are telling you, "No matter what, don't have sex!"

The key then is to discover sexual values which are based on lasting truth rather than changing opinions.

 LIFELINE

Truth vs. Opinion

Whose idea was it to have sexuality be so important? Read the following verses to find out where the whole issue of male and female relationships began: Genesis 1:26-28; 2:18-25.

☞   [**HINT: You may want to divide the group into smaller clusters for these discussion questions. The key is to have your group members in a setting in which they are comfortable to share their answers without pressure to "say the right thing."**]

Consider the following questions:

Why did God create both man and woman?

What type of relationship did God intend for Adam and Eve to have?

Read the following verses to discover how God views sexual relationships outside of the uniting of a man to a woman as marriage partners:

☞   [**HINT: These short reading sections can be read by you or by taking turns within the group. The latter is**

preferred because it produces a more active involvement among the group members.]

Proverbs 5:1-6, 18-20; 6:24-29; Galatians 5:19-21.

Consider the following questions:

What is God's view of the sexual relationship between a man and his wife?

What is God's view of the sexual relationship between a man and a woman who is not his wife?

God holds great esteem for His design of the sexual relationship between husband and wife. He views sex as more than something which is physical. Sexual intercourse is an intimately personal uniting of individuals, created by God for the sharing of not only bodies but minds, hearts, and souls as well.

This intimate bonding is an integral part of God's purpose for marriage. God created whole persons to experience sex in relationships which involve the whole person. Sexuality cannot be separated into just physical categories. It affects all of who a person is.

As we have seen in the simulated surveys, many people do not recognize God's design for sex in marriage. They do not accept His view that sexuality is a spiritual as well as a mental, emotional, and physical issue. In fact, some people seem to indicate that sexuality is only physical.

Pornography, for example, is one of the results of emphasizing sex as being physical rather than being related to the whole person. The result is a confusion of sensuality—the physical aspect of sex—with sexuality—our whole-person maleness or femaleness.

☞ **[HELP: Another important consideration is that most young people do not get involved sexually simply for the purpose of physical pleasure. Rather, adolescent sexual activity can also be traced back to needs for intimacy. As you discuss the sexual activity of their peers, keep in mind that young people do not perceive themselves as being lustful beings seeking only personal physical gratification. Neither should we perceive them as such, because they are not.**

We all need to realize, however, that the concept that true sexual needs can be met outside of God's design is just as much a lie as is pornography. Needs for love and intimacy are most often frustrated by teenage sexual experiences. Furthermore, any sexual involvement outside of a permanent commitment is settling for an inferior and temporary meeting of those needs, which ultimately does harm to not only the physical aspects of sexuality but the heart, soul, and mind as well.]

Sexual vs. Sensual

What does it mean to be sexual rather than sensual? Beside the following statements, write **SA** for strongly agree, **A** for agree, **?** for no opinion, **D** for disagree, and **SD** for strongly disagree.

_____ You must be sexually active in order to consider yourself to be truly sexual.

_____ Sexual intercourse is the uniting of two people in more than a physical union.

_____ It is sinful to be physically sexually attracted to another person.

_____ God disapproves of pornography.

_____ God does not care whether people have sex outside of marriage as long as they are happy and sharing love.

_____ Being sensually minded through exposure to pornography is an artificial and inferior way to have your sexual needs met.

____ Being sensually minded through sexual activity outside of marriage is an artificial and inferior way to have your sexual needs met.

____ Sexuality is created by God in each male and female. Sensuality is a lie against God's truth that He knows how to meet the needs of those whom He has created.

> Ask the group members to respond to individual answers and then point them back to the texts. Some questions they may raise may not be answered by these texts. You may even be unsure! That's OK! Those unanswered questions can be explored in the next few weeks. More important, you can model for them a willingness to grow and learn in your own understanding of these issues.

☞ [HINT: As you discuss the answers with the group members, obey the first rule of effective communication: LISTEN! You may want to jump in immediately and correct responses which are either unbiblical or confusing. However, group members need the freedom to express what they truly think and feel to be true without fear of being instantly told that they are right or wrong. They will be eager to hear your thoughts and to listen to your presentation of God's view once they realize that you believe that what they think and feel is valid even when you do not agree.]

 BODYLIFE

Applying the Truth to Public Opinion

Return to the list of statements in the survey. Based on what you have just studied and discussed, answer these two questions for each statement:

1. How would God respond to these statements?

2. What would be God's reasons for these responses?

☞ **[HINT: A true sign of growth by your group members is not the giving of the "right" answers as much as a desire to know more, a desire exhibited by asking the right questions.]**

God's Opinion: "Just Say Yes!"

"Just Say Yes!"? How can this first chapter in a series about sexuality and the Christian be entitled, "Just Say Yes!" God seems to be the main source of why we are supposed to say no to sex!

☞ **[HELP: "Just Say No!" was a major campaign of the late 1980s. The thrust of the message was to choose to say no to drug and alcohol abuse so that students would escape the harmful effects of such abuse.**

Because of the AIDS crisis, this same approach has been applied to the sexual decisions facing your group members. While the biblical message is: "Do not have sexual relations outside of the marital commitment," there is more to God's truth than "Just say no." Students may be surprised to find that God's view of sex and sexuality is not simply a focus on preventing sex, but is a means of providing for and protecting His children so that they find maximum fulfillment in who they are as male and female. The point is not just to "be good" but to be all God created them to be.]

The answer lies in what God has created us for and called us to as His children. God calls us to say yes to who we are sexually by saying no to sensuality, which is a false way to meet our sexual needs. God intended for us to experience sex in the context of a relationship of permanent commitment because sex involves all of who we are. God commands us to abstain from sex outside of this commitment of marriage because He knows we were not made for temporary sensual pleasure at the expense of our heart, mind, and soul. He knows that the sensual pleasure of sex is best within the total marital commitment of heart, mind, and soul.

☞ **[HINT: If you previously led this group through the Small Group Study** *Why Not Love All of Me?* **you may want to refer back to some of the teachings found in that material.]**

Life Response

To summarize the basis for this series, let's work together to write a clear, concise statement of what we understand God's will to be.

From God's point of view:
SEXUALITY is. . . .

SENSUALITY is. . . .

God therefore calls His children to say yes to. . . .

and no to. . . .

☞ **[HELP: It is not necessary to expect a commitment from group members at this point. The key here is that they understand the difference between sexuality and sensuality. Throughout this study you want to be able to affirm them as sexual beings created in God's image. This is the basis for saying yes.**

It will also become the basis for choosing to say no to the sensual temptations which surround them and appeal to their physical and relational desires.]

Perhaps you have been or are now sexually active. God's holiness and grace apply to you as much as to someone who has not made these choices. God's holiness calls you to seek, learn, and follow His will. His grace offers forgiveness, healing, and restoration. Philippians 3:12-14 teaches us that we can always move forward in Christ. You will also want to find others to provide support, reassurance, and comfort as you work through giving God control over your sexual decision-making.

If you have experienced the pain of rape or other sexual abuse, God has a message of healing, restoration, and freedom for you. Seek a listening, loving person with whom you can share your hurt and heart. You do not have to be controlled by the sins someone has committed against you.

In all things, no matter how painful or difficult, nothing can separate you from the love of God.

☞ **[HELP: A vital part of this series will be for you to model God's grace, as some of your group members may have already been sexually active. Be sensitive to the fact that some students feel there is no point in attempting sexual purity since they cannot regain their virginity. It is also possible that some have been sexually abused. These youth need to know that they are not "damaged goods" and that God's grace is sufficient for a restoration of sexual purity, though there may be some painful emotional consequences as a result of their sin or the sins of those who victimized them.]**

☞ **[HELP: In addition to the LIFE RESPONSE, your group may be ready for some follow-through activities. The following additional LIFE RESPONSES are ways in which your group members can practically apply this content in preparation for their next group sharing time:**

1. Pray for one another daily during this important study.

2. Make a list of movies or televison shows or commercials that emphasize or portray sex as being merely sensual.

3. Read 1 Thessalonians 4 prior to the next group session so that students will understand more of the context for God's commands for sexual purity.

4. Write out questions (perhaps anonymously at this point) about sex and sexuality which members would like to discuss as this series develops.

5. Invite a counselor or social worker who is a Christian to come to the group to discuss the negative effects he or she has witnessed as a result of pornography, sexual abuse, promiscuity, and sexual experimentation. This would reinforce that sex is much more than a physical experience.]

☞ [HINT: All the follow-through assignments in this series may be given as mere suggestions to group members or as actual assignments they are asked to commit to as a part of the group. Your approach will depend on the maturity and commitment level of the group. If you do have group members making serious commitments to do additional LIFE RESPONSES, be certain that you include follow-up in the subsequent group experience. As a leader, you model the importance of their commitments, as well as how to deal with failure to meet those expectations, by the way you work through the follow-up.]

What's Next?
"What's Love Got to Do with It?"—What is your response to the provision and protection God has designed for you sexually?

▼

What's Love Got to Do with It?

SESSION OVERVIEW

Purpose:

"What's Love Got to Do with It?" moves group members into a deeper personal exploration of God's design for expressing their God-given sexuality. The last session together brought group members to an understanding of what God has to say about saying yes to sexuality. During this time together, group members are challenged to write out a personal response to God's call for sexual purity.

Needs:

"If it feels good, do it" is a saying which came out of the 1970s. This phrase reflected the extent to which hedonism had invaded our culture. If the 1980s were any indication of where we are headed, it will only be getting worse.

Adolescents are especially susceptible to this type of value structure because of their intense and quickly changing emotions. Nowhere is this more evident than in the sexual realm. It is essential that adolescents be given an opportunity to objectively step back from the culture, their parents' expectations, and their peer influences to examine what

God has called them to in terms of obedience.

This small group can be the place where students make lifetime decisions about who they will choose to be for God's glory, submitting all of who they are, including their sexuality, to the love of the Father.

Goals:
The *leader's* goals include
(1) guiding group members in their evaluation of why people choose to be sexually active;
(2) encouraging group members to submit to God's will, responding to His love as their value base, and;
(3) enabling group members to express their intention to love God through their sexual decision-making processes.

The *group members'* goals are that they will be able
(1) to elaborate the principles of love behind the standards of God's holiness;
(2) to express a personal decision in terms of God's will for their sexual purity.

Life Response:
Group members will write out a personal response to God's loving command of provision and protection that His children remain sexually pure.

Resource Materials:
____ copies of *Where Do You Think Sex Came From?*
____ pens
____ Bibles

HEARTBEAT

☞ [HINT: Be certain to introduce anyone who was not with the group for the first meeting. It is essential that everyone feel welcomed, accepted, and affirmed by the rest of the group if an atmosphere of honest sharing is to be produced. It would also be an excellent idea to review last week's LIFE RESPONSE as well as the results of any additional LIFE RESPONSES.]

☞ [HELP: Prayer is an essential element of small group ministries. The power for growth and maturity in individual lives as well as within the group as a whole comes from the power of God's Spirit as He responds to our seeking God's will. Be certain that you are praying for the small group on a regular basis between meetings together. Also, you will want to include prayer either in the beginning or the end (or both!) in order to keep yourself and the students focused on the source of power required to "just say yes."]

☞ [HINT: Just a reminder: Always begin small group times with group members sitting comfortably in a circle so that eye contact can be made between each person in the group. Also, it is important to affirm each answer given by group members. These two elements are essential as you seek to facilitate community and bond-building within the group.]

Who Needs a Heart?

"What's Love Got to Do with It?" was a song made popular by Tina Turner and the movie *Mad Max: Beyond Thunderdome.* If you listen closely to the lyrics, you pick up the theme that relationships, particularly as they involve sex, are better off without love because love only leads to being hurt.

We live in a world where a lot of people have been hurt because of what was at one time considered to be a relationship of love. Because of this "getting burned," individuals are tempted to develop this cynical attitude of "Who needs a heart when a heart can be broken?"

Still, most people who are sexually involved do desire love from the relationship. The term "making love" is even used to describe sexual intercourse. This group time together will focus on the question, "What's love got to do with it?" when we respond to God's created design in the area of sexual decision-making.

Why Not? Why?
Let's quickly brainstorm on the following topics.

First: What are some reasons, other than out of obedience to God's will, that your peers do not become sexually active?

☞   [HINT: Brainstorming is a method of discovery learning whereby group members call out all that they can think of in response to a question. This is done without the leader or the members taking time to evaluate the correctness of the responses. Let each group member call out ideas, list them, and take time to discuss them only after you have completed the brainstorming activity. The brainstorming should be just like popping popcorn—stop when things start slowing down.]

Second: What are some reasons that your peers do become sexually active?

Using these lists as a starting point, we will now divide into two groups for a debate. We will debate the pros and cons of why a teenager should choose to be sexually active. It does not matter whether you agree with the position of your group at this time; the point is just to make the best possible argument for your side of the debate. [One other note should be added: This is to be done without reference to being a Christian or obeying God. This is from a strictly secular perspective.]

☞ [HINT: The reason for forcing group members to prepare a point of view which may not be their own and may not be biblical is two-fold:

1. Group members will be challenged to think through a number of different perspectives rather than simply giving answers which they think would be expected in a Bible study context.

2. Group members are given an opportunity to see the difference in merely reasoning from a human perspective and truly basing decisions on the Word of God.]

The topic of the debate is: RESOLVED: Teenagers should feel free to become sexually active as soon as they feel they are ready.

The format should be similar to the following:

The affirmative side will argue for two minutes on why the resolved statement is the best perspective.

The negative side will then respond with its own two-minute argument against teenagers' becoming sexually active.

Following these opening arguments, each side will be given three minutes to prepare a one-minute rebuttal.

Prepare group members by informing them that they will be given an opportunity to share their true thoughts and feelings about this topic following the debate. Encourage them to listen to things which are said which they agree or disagree with during the debate.

Give each side 8–10 minutes to prepare a 2-minute

argument for their side. You will umpire the debate based on their arguments. Encourage them to use examples and persuasive points. Remind them that the issue is not whether they agree or disagree with their side; the point is to prepare the best possible argument.

After the debate it will be important to let individuals voice their own opinions about this subject. At this point allow them to interject their priority to do God's will. Group members need to understand that arriving at truth is not just a matter of weighing pros and cons. Making a decision must include what God has to say about the subject. This will reinforce last week's content and prepare them for what is ahead in this study.

Two cautions should be noted:

One, prepare the group members not to take any of their arguments personally or to use personal attacks as a part of the debate. This discussion, as with any good debate, is about the issue only.

Second, maintain the tension between the two sides. If they pick up from you that you are just going to side with the negative and not listen to the affirmative, then one side will feel defeated before they begin. The point of having this debate is to see some of the issues which they will be facing if they choose God's will for their sexuality.

☞ [HINT: Preparing debates with younger adolescents may require adult leadership to organize and focus their ideas. Keep the maturity factor of your group in mind when you use this method.]

Finally, as a group, let's express our views on this topic.

Allow the group to discuss together their individual and corporate opinions. It would be helpful to ask them to express what they agreed or disagreed with from each side of the debate.

LIFELINE
God's Plan: Protection and Provision

God does not have a negative view of sex. He created sex! He, as a loving Father, knows what is best for you sexually and He wants what is best for you.

In our last group time we emphasized that sex is much more than a physical act—it affects the whole person. In this study we will examine more specifically the call to respond to God's design for sexual relationships.

Let's read 1 Thessalonians 4:1-8. Write out the key statements that reveal what God the Father's will is for His children.

☞ [HINT: You may want to do this in smaller groups so that you get a number of different perspectives on the passage.]

God the Father has a high view of the intensity of sexual desire. Let's read 1 Corinthians 7:1-6. Paul was writing at a time of great persecution. He encouraged believers not to marry if they were still single, but recognized that singleness would be too difficult for some. This passage reflects God's provision of marriage for the fulfillment of sexual desire.

God the Father has a high view of sexual intercourse within marriage. Read Hebrews 13:4. Let's write a brief paraphrase of this verse.

God the Father also has a high view of His children as whole persons. Read 1 Corinthians 6:15-20. Let's write a brief paraphrase of verses 17 and 18.

Let's briefly consider the following questions based on the verses we have read:

1. What does following God's will of sexual purity provide for an individual?

2. What does following God's will of sexual purity protect an individual from?

It Works in Real Life

During your lifetime you will often see how God shows His love through His design for sexual intercourse as an expression of marital commitment only. Below are true examples of Christian teenagers who have had to experience what happens when they stepped outside of God's will in expressing sexuality. The names and events have been slightly altered, but each account remains true to the type of experiences God wants to protect His children from.

☞ **[HINT: Have individuals read these true stories aloud to the group.]**

● Belinda was an active member of her church youth group and was considered a fun, attractive person with many talents. During her sophomore year of high school she began dating William, a senior in the youth group. They dated for about six months, gradually becoming more and more physically involved until they had begun having intercourse.

After about two years of dating William, Belinda decided that God did know what was best for her. She decided to drop the relationship with William and offer her life to God to be used by Him in serving others for Christ. She broke off the relationship and began seeking ways to prepare herself for the future God had for her. Belinda experienced God's forgiveness and renewal. However, she also had to experience the consequences of what she had done outside of God's will. Just before she broke up with William, she discovered she was pregnant.

God never stopped loving Belinda, and she loved Him as well. Now she is rearing a child on her own, however, rather than doing what she had planned for her future.

• Lyle and Kristen had been dating for two years. They really loved each other and intended to be married one day. Both believed that God had brought them together. They eagerly anticipated being married, rearing a family, and enjoying God's blessings in their relationship.

Despite repeated commitments to back off their physical involvement, they found themselves having intercourse on a fairly regular basis. They felt guilty after each time, yet they just seemed to get caught up in the moment and lose control.

Kristen became pregnant, and they were faced with a very difficult decision. Because they loved each other and still wanted to do God's will, they chose to get married immediately and begin their family early. This caused a great deal of stress between Lyle and Kristen. It also affected their families. There were many regrets because they chose not to obey God. They often wished that they could have been free of all these strains and pressures.

God lovingly enabled them to make it through those first tough years and later provided another child. Lyle and Kristen are, however, still feeling the effects of their decisions years later.

• Benjamin struggled with his Christian faith all during high school. He often went into denial about God, ignoring

God's Word and pretending God did not care what he did.

A part of pretending God was distant from him included becoming sexually involved with his girlfriend. This lasted for about six months. When she broke up with him, he turned to God with his hurt, and, for the last two years, has been working to deepen his relationship with his heavenly Father.

Now, two years later, he has begun dating Annie. Annie is everything Benjamin could ever have dreamed of having in a girlfriend. Both want to go to the mission field some day and both dream of adopting children who are unwanted because of their age or disabilities. The relationship has been growing rapidly for the last two months and it seems to everyone, including Annie, to be an ideal relationship. The problem is that when Benjamin is kissing Annie, he begins thinking about his former sexual relationship. He feels awful for even thinking of Annie in this way. Those images of the past are like etchings which have been engraved on his mind.

He also feels very sad because he is certain that Annie is a virgin. Although he is confident that she will forgive his past as God has forgiven him, how he wishes he had kept himself for her the way she has remained pure. He knows that if he does marry Annie one day, he will always regret what occurred in his sexual relationship of the past.

Even more scary is the fear that Benjamin will take a long time to overcome his weakness in his lustful thoughts about Annie, whom he wants to see only with God's purity. He knows he can trust God, but it is very painful for him.

• Amy has been plagued for two years with bouts of depression and anxiety. She has struggled greatly because she feels inadequate, inferior, and unlovable. She knows these thoughts are contrary to who she is in Christ. However, her feelings overwhelm her biblical thinking at times and she is left almost hating herself.

These feelings and thoughts began when Luke broke off their relationship. After dating for one and half years they began to be sexually involved. Amy knew it was not exactly right, but she rationalized that they were so in love and since they would almost certainly one day be married, God would not mind. When Luke told her that he just did not love her any more only two months later, all of Amy's self-esteem and hope seemed to leave with him. Her relationship with God, once intimate and growing, now seemed empty. The life with Luke which she had planned as the source of her happiness and the basis of her becoming sexually active with him was now gone forever.

Through friends and a Christian youth leader, Amy is finding a way to put the pieces back together. But she still wonders if she will ever be able to truly trust a guy in a personal relationship again.

 BODYLIFE

The Father's Will
Let's divide into small "cell groups" of two or three persons. In these groups prepare a position on the topic we debated, only this time from God's point of view. Write a one-sentence statement and develop your reasons for defending it. (Remember to include God's design to provide and protect.)

☞ **[HELP: Highlight God's motivation of love and holiness in giving commands for sexual purity.]**

Life Response
Write out your personal response to God's command for sexual purity. Include how you feel about His design, what

you intend to do as a result of this command, and what you need from Him as your Father.

☞ **[HELP: Encourage group members to be honest with God about these responses. Meaningless commitments are more harmful than helpful. Some group members may not be ready to truly commit themselves to obeying God. Others may have more questions. Perhaps most, and maybe all, will be ready to accept God's provision and protection of sexual purity.**

Be sensitive to the individual who has sinned by having become sexually active. While emphasizing that there are always consequences to violating God's will, be sure also to point out His abundant grace and healing power.]

☞ **[HELP: Additional LIFE RESPONSES:**

1. Hold a group study on the consequences of sexual immorality found in the Bible (for example, David).

2. Find resources on the statistics which have been compiled about teenage pregnancy, abortion, AIDS. . . .

3. Commit to sharing the above LIFE RESPONSE with parents or significant other adults.

4. Commit to sharing the above LIFE RESPONSE with the dating partners of those who are in steady relationships.]

☞ **[HINT: When making these types of commitments, be certain that group members are actively involved. We don't want to just ask them if they will do this so that their investment in the initial commitment is to merely say yes. We want them to meaningfully affirm this commitment before God and one another. In this way they are witnesses together of the importance of the commitment they are making and their serious intention to keep it.]**

☞ [HELP: Your group members may be at various places in respect to their commitments at this point. This will have a bearing on whether or not they are ready for additional LIFE RESPONSES. It will be important to continue to develop accountability relationships that will encourage and support those individuals who make commitments.

Follow-up is an essential aspect of accountability. No one will condemn the group member who has not fulfilled his or her commitment. At the same time, this type of commitment cannot be taken so lightly that it does not matter if members do fail to fulfill it. You will need to consider the best approach for your group in terms of accountability.]

What's Next?
"How Far Is Too Far?"—How do you know how much physical involvement is too much? What are considered to be Christian standards?

▼

THREE

How Far Is Too Far?

SESSION OVERVIEW

Purpose:

"How Far Is Too Far?" encourages group members to think through dating standards that are appropriate for the Christian who desires to be sexually pure. This session challenges group members not only to do what is right in abstaining from immorality but to develop a personal attitude of commitment to be all God created them to be.

Needs:

Many times Christian youth rationalize about what is appropriate in a dating relationship. They will even say, "Well, the Bible only says not to have intercourse. It does not say anything about other types of sexual activities."

Some of this type of reasoning does come from confusion and misunderstanding. At other times, however, a young person tries to get away with being sensual without feeling as guilty as if he or she had been having sex.

Group members need, therefore, to have correct information, accurate understanding of the issues involved, and a specific challenge to submit to God's will for their sexuality.

Goals:

The *leader's* goals include

(1) helping group members identify what they currently perceive to be acceptable physical involvement in dating relationships;

(2) guiding group members in moving from biblical principles to specific, practical applications;

(3) enabling group members to make commitments to standards of physical involvement with dating partners.

The *group members'* goals are

(1) to evaluate their current standards and/or practices of physical contact with dates;

(2) to understand God's view of what is appropriate;

(3) to develop personal guidelines of conduct for dating.

Life Response:

Group members will write down where they are going to place their "physical boundary" line. They will also write a brief prayer thanking God for His creation of their sexuality and for His provision and protection as a Father.

Resource Materials:

____ copies of *Where Do You Think Sex Came From?*

____ pens

____ Bibles

____ food for opening activity

HEARTBEAT

Begin this group time with an activity which is guaranteed to interest the young people and which will also set up discovery learning in this group time.

Serve some kind of food which the young people will enjoy. It should be something they really like (e.g., brownies, pizza, candy, cookies). Second, it should be more than at least most of them could possibly want to eat of this particular food. (You may have to be creative if you have a group of real eaters.)

You will refer to this activity when the "Law of Diminishing Returns" is discussed later in the meeting.

How Far?

"How far should a person go with physical affection?" is a common concern for students who are dating. God's will for sexual purity has been made clear in our two previous meetings. The standard is virginity until marriage and faithfulness to one's spouse after marriage.

Because sexual intercourse has been termed "going all the way," the phrase "going too far" has naturally followed. Typically, "going too far" has meant doing something which is beyond a person's boundaries of what is right in his or her physical relationship. Because the Bible has little to say about kissing and does not even mention what we call "petting," the natural question is, "How far is too far?"

That's Far Enough

Following is a continuum of physical contact which could take place between a guy and a girl. Mark an **X** where most of the non-Christians you know would place the boundary line of how far to go. Mark an **O** where the Christians you know would draw the line.

- holding hands

- arm around shoulder

- goodnight kiss

- prolonged kiss

- prolonged kiss while in passionate embrace

- kissing while touching one another outside of clothes for sexual arousal

- kissing while touching one another inside of clothes for sexual arousal (breasts, genital areas)

- kissing and touching while naked

- stimulating one another to orgasm without actually having intercourse

- having sexual intercourse

☞ **[HINT: For various reasons group members may be tentative about talking about this issue. They may feel embarrassed, guilty, or confused by the discussion. For this reason, the questions focus on what others think, not what they think about the issue.**

Dividing into same-sex groups may be appropriate and help your students feel more comfortable.]

Based purely on what has been discussed the past two weeks, where do you think God would place the boundaries for His children? Explain your reasons for this boundary line.

 LIFELINE

Christian Sexuality: Biblical Principles

Because the Bible does not specifically address all the above issues, let's examine Scripture for principles which can be applied to dating guidelines.

1. James 1:13-15.

List the process by which we move into temptation and then into an area of sin.

This process is a progression by which we gradually find ourselves choosing our way over God's way. What is good from God is lost in what we want for ourselves that is outside God's will.

2. Romans 6:12-13.

What are the negative commands in these verses?

What are the positive commands in these verses?

The choice to not give into our lusts begins with yielding

our bodies to God to be used for His glory and for the accomplishment of His will.

3. 1 Corinthians 6:12-20.

Rewrite verse 12 in a contemporary paraphrase.

What is the principle of verses 19-20?

In this text, part of which we examined in relationship to God's protection and provison for sexual intercourse, we find that the body belongs to God and that the issue is not "What can I get away with?" but, rather, "What can I do to bring glory to Him?"

To summarize:
- Lust leads us away from God in order to fulfill our desires.
- Our bodies should be yielded to God for His glory.
- Our bodies belong to God, and we should view ourselves and one another in this way.

Christian Sexuality: Natural Principles
There are also some important principles not found in the Bible which will contribute to our understanding of how to apply the above truths to dating relationships.

1. The Principle of Diminishing Returns. The first bite of that food you have been craving tastes better than anything you can remember. The first 10 bites are exhilarating. The next 10 are pretty good. By about 30 or 40 bites, however, much of the initial thrill is gone. You can only eat so much of a good thing until it turns out to be not so good any more.

☞ [HELP: Point out the leftovers from the food you served at the beginning of the group session. Your students will recognize that if they had eaten all the food available, they would be feeling pretty sick. In our sex-saturated society, far more sensual experience is available than is healthy for them.]

2. The Principle of Opposing Forces. Suppose you are sitting at a red traffic signal. You are waiting impatiently for a light which never seems to change. In the process of waiting you have your left foot pushing the brake to the floor. At the same time you have your right foot pushing the accelerator to the floor. The car is in gear. This means that sooner or later (probably sooner) one force will give way to the other.

3. The Principle of Sexual Arousal. God designed sexual intercourse to be pleasurable. He made man and woman's bodies in such a way that they need to experience a time of preparation prior to actual intercourse. This time prepares the body for maximum pleasure and stimulation during sex.

Because of this design there are ways of touching one another and embracing one another which are termed "foreplay." This foreplay enables the couple to prepare not only physically but also emotionally and mentally for the fulfillment of an intimate personal union.

If "foreplay" is engaged in without this fulfillment, it leads to frustration, anxiety, and often mistrust. If sex occurs without this foreplay, the same results can occur. Sexual arousal through foreplay and sexual intercourse are, therefore, inseparable in God's design.

Putting It Together
As a group, let's see if we can find a correlation between these three principles and the Scriptural principles we discovered earlier.

How does the **Principle of Diminishing Returns** relate to physical involvement in dating?

☞ **[HELP: The more physically involved you become, the quicker you will be ready to move into the next level of involvement. Holding hands is a rush the first time you do it. After a while you begin kissing, etc.]**

How can this progression create a problem with lust which could lead to sin (as we saw in James 1:13-17)?

☞ **[HELP: Spending too much time displaying physical affection can lead to the desire to go on to the next level. Even if you feel you have everything under control, over a period of time it becomes increasingly difficult to maintain that control.**

   Thus intense involvement at any level can be like throwing gasoline on coals that are still hot even though you no longer see a flame. Pretty soon you are playing with fire!]

How does the **Principle of Opposing Forces** relate to physical involvement in dating?

☞ **[HELP: If you are trying to remain physically pure while also trying to do as much as you can physically without actually getting sexually involved, one of the two forces will eventually take control.]**

How can this create a problem with lust which could lead to sin?

☞ **[HELP: The more you feed the physical, the stronger the physical desire becomes. The more you feed the spiritual, the stronger the spiritual desire becomes.]**

Too often young people try to "get away with" as much as

they can without going "all the way." There are two key problems with this.

First, many things which are not actually sexual intercourse are sexually intimate. Therefore, you can become sensual and miss out on God's design for sexual purity without actually having intercourse.

Second, the more you focus on the physical, the more control it begins to take in the relationship. Eventually spiritual commitments can be overridden by the immediacy of physical desire.

As we can see, young people who find themselves in these types of relationships are not really "getting away" with anything, instead they are forfeiting something very valuable.

How does the **Principle of Sexual Arousal** relate to the fact that our bodies are God's and must be yielded to Him for His glory?

☞ **[HELP: Our bodies belong to God sexually, not only in the sense that He is glorified by our abstaining from sexual intercourse outside of marriage, but also in the sense that every expression of our sexuality should be according to His design. Sexual arousal which was created for preparation for intercourse should be confined to the marriage relationship where that arousal can be fulfilled according to God's design.**

 BODYLIFE

God's Design and Boundary Line
After this study, look back at the continuum. Where do you think God would place the boundary line for dating relationships?

☞ **[HINT: Group members may have different answers at this point. Be sure to refer to the biblical and natural principles as you facilitate this discussion. Encourage group members to talk freely while being prepared to interject truth for the purpose of correcting misunderstanding and errors.**

It is vital that group members realize that while there is some room for debate on what is wise in terms of kissing and embracing, it is clear that petting is a dangerous physical involvement and there are adequate biblical principles to conclude that this is not glorifying to God except as a part of the foreplay of marital intercourse.]

The best preparation for intimate sexual relations in marriage according to God's design is to yield yourself to God now. Thus, it becomes important to develop personal standards based on God's truth as to where you will draw the boundary line.

One thing you should consider in drawing this line for yourself is that you are best advised not to draw the line at its maximum point of "safety." In other words, based on what we have studied, if you draw your boundary line at the farthest possible point before you are violating God's design for you sexually, you run a higher risk of crossing that line at some point. Because of the importance of this issue, it is wisest to draw the line in such a way that, were you to make a mistake, you still would not have lost a very precious gift from God.

Remember, God's will is for your provision and protection.

Life Response
Write down where you are going to place your "physical boundary" line. Along with this commitment, write a brief

prayer thanking God for His creation of your sexuality and for His provision and protection for you.

☞ **[HELP: Additional optional LIFE RESPONSES:**

1. Ask group members to openly share their prayers and/or boundary line commitments.

2. Help group members develop a list of creative dates which would support rather than work against their standards.

3. Have a panel discussion with parents to discuss the process and guidelines and how to help.

4. Ask a married couple who kept strong commitments to sexual purity to share with the group how God blessed their decision.

5. Ask someone who did not keep such a strong commitment, but has since submitted himself or herself to God's will, to share what he or she has learned about God's protection and provision as well as His forgiving grace.]

What's Next?

"Remote Control"—Once you have a boundary line, how do you control sexual desire so that the desire does not control you?

▼

Remote Control

SESSION OVERVIEW

Purpose:

"Remote Control" will enable group members to understand the process of developing self-control, specifically as it relates to sexuality. Group members are challenged to choose to take control of their lives rather than waiting for circumstances or events to be the primary influence in their sexual decision-making process. Self-control is remote control because group members are seeking to prepare for successfully keeping the boundaries they have set, though the actual practicing of those boundaries may still be in the future.

Needs:

Adolescents are susceptible to being swayed by momentary circumstances and feelings. This results from not having developed the mature personal and interpersonal resources required for maintaining long-term goals and commitments.

To assist group members in becoming mature, we begin by helping them understand the cause-and-effect relationship between the decisions they make now and the persons they become later. Group members need to perceive themselves more accurately as not having to wait for self-control to simply happen, but rather as being active participants in nurturing self-control for both the present and future.

Self-control is a fruit of the Spirit, which can be cultivated through the renewing of the mind and the submission of the will to God. Group members, therefore, can begin to develop self-control from a position of strength in the Holy Spirit if they belong to Christ.

Goals:

The *leader's* goals include

(1) helping group members identify their own levels of self-control;

(2) enabling group members to understand how they can overcome exterior control by developing internal self control;

(3) assisting group members in setting up a personal plan of decision-making which will develop maturity.

The *group members'* goals are

(1) to honestly evaluate their strengths and weaknesses in self-control issues;

(2) to discover specific ways in which they can develop self-control.

Life Response:

Group members will write a list of ways in which they can personally be renewed through exposure to, experience with, and expression of God's will as it relates to their personal sexuality.

Resource Materials:

___ copies of *Where Do You Think Sex Came From?*

___ Bibles

___ pens

HEARTBEAT

Self-Control

The discussion was on maintaining one's virginity until marriage. One member of the youth group, a 16-year-old guy, shared this with the group: "I know what I should do. But I am not sure I can make it. I just don't know how much longer I can wait."

For most group members it is a long time between their sexual maturity in the early teenage years and marriage, which usually occurs in the middle 20s. With the increase of sexual desire, the influence of a culture that always seems to be writing and talking about sex, and the deepening of intimacy of dating relationships, it can be difficult to keep those goals and guidelines which have been set. Like most of life's commitments, it is easier said than done.

So, how can you know in advance that you will be successful? The answer is by developing a godly self-control. This group meeting will focus on "Remote Control" as we try to prepare for a future of successful decision-making.

I Can't Help Myself

How is your self-control at this point? Place the letter of each area of control at the appropriate place on the scale below.

(Can't Control)   (Can Control)
     1—2—3—4—5—6—7—8—9—10

A. Eating a dessert or junk food just because it is there
B. Staying up too late when you know you should go to bed
C. Saving money

D. Not procrastinating with school work
E. Getting household chores done without being told
F. Watching what you say—controlling your tongue
G. Dealing with anger
H. Watching TV shows or movies you know are not worthwhile

What makes it difficult for you to have self-control in specific areas?

What are some of the things which make it difficult for your peers to have self-control in the area of sexuality?

 **LIFELINE**

Remote Control

Let's read Romans 12:1-2. Write this verse in a paraphrase which applies each command and principle to the area of sexual decision-making.

We are transformed by the renewing of our mind, which results *from* our yielding ourselves to God and results *in* our doing His will. God is our greatest resource for doing His will—He has provided the resources.

Let's read Galatians 5:22-23. What do these verses teach us about self-control?

We have a Father who supplies the resources we need for renewal and self-control. We can trust God for future control as long as we are working to submit ourselves to Him to be transformed in our minds and to be filled with His Spirit in our heart and soul.

So, how do we submit ourselves for remote control? Before we answer, let's read together two examples of loss of control.

#1 The Diet

Joe had finally begun the diet he had planned to start for months. It was only six weeks until basketball season and he needed to lose at least 10 pounds in order to be ready for those killer running drills. Joe committed himself to eating only three meals a day with no desserts. All sweets and between-meal snacks were off-limits.

Today he walked by the local ice cream parlor. Joe was used to eating about a quart of ice cream, his favorite food, each day. Inside the store were Jimmy, Carol, Suzanne, and Paul, all close friends. They were eating and laughing, and Joe thought he should go in and say hello.

He knew he should not eat any ice cream, but it would not hurt to be in the store. However, feeling kind of funny about being the only person not eating ice cream, he decided to order some just to be a part of the group. He did not plan on eating. He planned to just let the others eat what he ordered.

After he ordered a banana split with nuts, whipped cream, and a cherry (his favorite), he sat down with his friends. He was not going to eat any of the ice cream, but he went ahead and got a spoonful just to feel better. The longer he sat there, the closer the spoon full of ice cream, syrup, and whipped cream came to his mouth. He could smell the chocolate sauce and could almost taste the rich, creamy ice cream he so longed for.

With this delicious treat staring him in the face, Joe thought to himself, "I need to make an objective decision about whether or not I should eat this one bite of ice cream."

What do you think happened to Joe's banana split? Sound ridiculous? Consider the following illustration:

50

#2 **The Date**

Joe and Sherry had been dating for several months. Both were regular attenders of church youth groups and they came from Christian homes. They never talked about what their boundary was in their physical relationship, and thus far it had been gradually progressing. Both had just assumed that they would not have sexual intercourse, though neither was certain how far they would go.

On Friday, Joe picked up Sherry for the prom. He was in a limo! Joe was striking in his black tuxedo and Sherry was stunning in her white prom dress. Joe thought Sherry was the sexiest girl he had ever seen. Sherry felt like Joe was treating her like a queen with the limo, the beautiful orchid corsage, and his gentlemanly manners.

That night was the perfect date for both of them. During the slow dance, they kissed, and Sherry thought of how she wanted this night to last forever. Joe had never felt closer to Sherry than this night. He knew he wanted to marry this girl one day.

After the prom, Joe surprised Sherry by taking her back to his house. His parents were already asleep, and in the downstairs den by the fireplace he had prepared a candlelight midnight snack, complete with a rose and soft music. Sherry almost cried when she saw all that Joe had done to prepare this romantic mood. Joe and Sherry just held each other for a long while as they both said, "I love you." They were each sure that the other really meant this. Soon they became quite physically involved and lost in the romance. Suddenly, Joe pulled back from Sherry and said, "We need to make an objective decision about our physical relationship, Sherry."

Right! No way are Joe and Sherry going to be objective at this moment.

Many people try to make decisions about their sexuality in times of intense emotional and physical attraction. Objectivity may be beyond their ability at that point.

"Remote Control" is thinking ahead so that self-control is developed and maintained. Joe and Sherry may be able to avoid making serious mistakes in their physical relationship. More likely, without actually planning to do so, they will cross over into a harmful level of involvement with one another. Let's examine what they could have done to have prepared themselves for self-control.

The 3-E Control Pattern

We can develop "remote control" by using the following pattern: EXPOSURE – EXPERIENCE – EXPRESSION.

EXPOSURE – Exposing ourselves to God's will through His Word, prayer, Christian fellowship, and godly examples of other believers.

EXPERIENCE – Experiencing the positive results of relationships that are glorifying to God. Spending time and energy in developing those areas in which we do not struggle with self-control and do enjoy God's will.

EXPRESSION – Expressing God's will by making decisions which will strengthen our commitment to Him and His will. Doing what is necessary to insure our success in obeying Him.

How could Joe and Sherry have practiced this pattern for their physical relationship?

 BODYLIFE
Planning For Success!
God is faithful as we submit ourselves to Him. If we follow

this pattern of remote control, He will provide the renewal we need to continue in His will.

The EXPOSURE—EXPERIENCE—EXPRESSION pattern works in the negative as well, however. In other words, if you begin to expose yourself to, experience, and express things which are not according to His will, you are leading yourself away from God toward sensuality. What are some of the negative ways this pattern can develop?

Life Response
Write out for yourself a short plan of action according to the 3-E pattern. This will serve as your commitment to submit yourself to God so that He will renew your mind and fill your being with His Spirit.

☞   [HELP: Additional optional LIFE RESPONSES:
   1. Share this commitment with adults he or she is accountable to.
   2. Share this commitment with the person he or she is dating.
   3. Become accountable to the group by planning to discuss the same matters in future serious relationships.
   4. Ask college-age students who have godly dating relationships how they maintain self-control.]

What's Next?
"Depressurization"—How do you rely on your self-control when you are facing crowd control?

▼

Depressurization

SESSION OVERVIEW

Purpose:

"Depressurization" provides group members with practical skills necessary for dealing with peer pressure in the area of sexuality. Group members are given an opportunity to learn how to counteract external pressures with an internal confidence that is greater than anything or anyone who might try to influence them and sway their commitment to submit their sexuality to God.

Having prepared themselves for a future of self-control, group members will examine ways to confidently respond to peers who are not supportive of their values.

Needs:

Adolescents need more than a commitment to do what is right before God. They also must be given the skills required to keep that commitment.

Their decisions to maintain sexual purity and to yield their bodies to God are exciting points of obedience. To continue that obedience as they mature into adults, adolescents need practical "how to's" that will enable them to overcome external threats to their internal stability. Without such skills, young people will be left frustrated and guilty, wondering why they are inadequate to do what is right before God.

Skills are learned through both formal and informal education. In other words, not only must group members have direct training in developing techniques for dealing with peer pressure, but they should also be able to observe and to interact with positive adult role models.

Goals:

The *leader's* goals include
(1) helping group members understand that they need certain skills in order to keep their commitments;
(2) affirming group members in their intention to overcome peer pressure;
(3) enabling group members to develop ways in which they can practically respond to this pressure.

The *group members'* goals are
(1) to develop a biblical attitude toward peer pressure;
(2) to develop practical responses to sexual peer pressure.

Life Response:

Group members will role play specific responses to peer pressure that will support them in expressing their sexuality according to God's design.

Resource Materials:

___ copies of *Where Do You Think Sex Came From?*
___ Bibles
___ pens

HEARTBEAT

The Pressure's On!

When submarines descend deep into the ocean, they encounter dramatic changes in the pressures surrounding them. A submarine would fold like tin foil from the weight of the water were it not for internal pressurization. The internal pressure must be equal to that on the outside, otherwise the external pressure will collapse the walls.

Much has been written and said about the peer pressure you and your friends are facing. Whether it's pressure to get involved in cheating in class, to begin drinking alcohol, or to blow off parental rules, each of us have watched friends at school crumble under the pressure of the crowd.

Most likely, we also have experienced negative peer pressure concerning sexuality in one form or another. How can one develop an internal strength which will stabilize this pressure? How can we avoid experiencing an internal "depressurization" when a date or peers seem to be closing in and pressuring our values?

Pressure Points

To begin this time together, let's brainstorm why peer pressure leads people to do things that they had not intended to do. What are the reasons your peers are influenced by the crowd?

☞ **[HINT: Remember, in brainstorming, students call out all that they can think of in response to a question. This is done without the leader or the group taking time to evaluate the correctness of the responses. Thus, let each student call out ideas, list them, and take time to discuss them only after you have completed the brain-**

storming activity. **Brainstorming should be like pop-**
ping popcorn—stop when things start slowing down.]

 **LIFELINE**

Bad Recordings

Two messages can be "played" through our minds as a result of peer pressure.

The first message is: "You are immature if you do not do this. It shows that you are afraid to live your own life." In the area of sexuality, the perception is that others think of you as being inadequate, childish, and so dependent on your parents or God that you are afraid to get involved like everyone else. You begin to feel like you are missing out on what it means to grow up and be sexually mature.

The second message is: "You are not the right kind of person. You are a loser who is going to be left out and left behind by your friends." In the area of sexuality, the perception is that you will lose your peer group of friends, perhaps even a current boyfriend or girlfriend, if you do not do the things they are doing. You begin to feel that you are going to be abandoned and alone if you do not become sexually active like the rest of your peers.

Changing the Messages

Let's look at the first message: "You are immature if you do not do this. It shows that you are afraid to live your own life."

How would you respond to this idea in relation to your maintaining a life of sexual purity?

In "cell groups" read the following verses and write out what God has to say about obeying Him instead of the crowd: Psalm 1; Proverbs 3:5-6.

☞ [HINT: When using these "cell group" questions, be certain that group members are either writing down their answers individually or they have a representative to record their corporate responses. The benefit of working together to examine a passage is lost if they do not keep track of what they are discovering.

After a report from the "cell groups" and a summary of what they have learned, move on to the next "cell group" activity.]

How would you respond to the second message: "You are not the right kind of person. You are a loser who is going to be left out and left behind by your friends?"

Once again, in our cell groups, let's read the following verses on Christian love and write out what God sees as the "right kind of person": 1 Corinthians 13:4-8; Colossians 3:12-17.

☞ [HINT: After a report from the cell groups and a summary of what group members have learned, move on to the next cell group activity.]

Finally, in your cell groups, read the following case study and discuss the questions which follow.

Case Study

Jan has been dating Dale for 10 months, longer than anyone she has ever dated. Jan thought everything was perfect between them until last Friday night.

The trouble started after they had just finished watching a movie and while they were involved in intimate kissing. Dale let Jan know that he felt that he was ready to have sex with her and that he wanted them to start thinking about birth control. Jan was shocked. She knew Dale had made a commitment to Christ two years ago and she just assumed that he shared her values concerning sexuality.

Jan and Dale eventually got into a huge fight. Dale insisted that all of the guys who were his friends were having sex with their girlfriends. Jan did not believe him, and they ended the fight with Jan telling Dale that she would prove him to be wrong.

Jan started talking with girls who were dating Dale's friends. To her surprise, most of them *were* having sex with their boyfriends. She also was surprised at how uncomfortable she was in talking with them about her relationship with Dale. At one point Jan caught herself feeling embarrassed about the fact that she and Dale were not sexually active. It seemed like these girls would look down on her or as if something were wrong with her for being a virgin. She kept remembering how Dale talked about some of the guys making fun of his virginity, and now she had an idea how he must feel.

Jan had promised herself that she would obey God and remain sexually pure for marriage. It seemed like it was going to cost her a relationship with Dale as well as the esteem of many of her friends. She began to feel that she was going to be alone if she kept her current values, but she also wondered what she'd be losing if she did not.

Questions to consider (briefly summarize your answers):
   1. How would you describe Dale's feelings at this point?

   2. How would you describe Jan's feelings at this point?

   3. What are the options Dale has in this situation?

   4. What are the options Jan has in this situation?

   5. How could Jan respond to the pressure she is feeling

in such a way that she would not be compromising her values?

6. What would be the possible negative and positive results of this action?

> **Following the cell group discussion, have the group members discuss their answers with the total group. Challenge them to be realistic about the difficulty of this situation. Try to move the discussion toward how they would feel and what they would consider doing in this situation.**

 BODYLIFE

Lines of Lies

Let's brainstorm to produce a list of the phrases or lines guys and girls used to convince others to be sexually active.

☞ **[HELP: For example: "If you loved me, you would let me." "It's time you became a man/woman." "We're not kids any more." "Everyone is doing it." "It will make our love stronger." "I really need you." "If you don't, I'm not sure our relationship can continue."]**

What should be your goal in responding to such lines?

☞ **[HELP: To communicate your confidence in your values concerning sex and to affirm God's design for your sexuality. Also, to use these responses as an opportunity to share your commitment to Christ.]**

Life Response

Let's role play possible ways to respond to these pressure statements. This skill will help us stay strong when we feel like we are facing a time of depressurization.

Take turns using two group members with each line. Have one person say the pressure line and then have the second person respond. Then let them play it out for a few moments, exploring some of the possible consequences of these types of responses. Keep the role plays brief to maintain momentum.

Debrief by discussing how group members felt during the role-play situations, how effective they thought the responses were, and what they would do in the future if they encountered such a pressure line.

☞   [HELP: Optional additional LIFE RESPONSES:
1. Commit to one another to be available for support during pressure times.
2. Write out specific responses to pressure lines and the biblical bases for these responses.
3. Memorize Scripture to counteract the negative messages of peer pressure.
4. Prepare a list of what you want in a true friendship to help you discern the false promises of peer pressure "friendship."]

What's Next?

"Stimulating Relationships" — How can you develop a base of support through positive peer influence that will be greater than negative peer pressure?

▼

SIX

Stimulating Relationships

SESSION OVERVIEW

Purpose:

"Stimulating Relationships" adds the final brush strokes to the portrait of a Christian attitude toward sex. Without loving, supporting friendships, the call to sexual purity is an incomplete picture. Your group members are challenged not only to be committed to Christ in regard to their own sexuality, but to take responsibility for encouraging one another as well. Group members will be given an opportunity to become enablers for one another, helping each one to honor his or her commitment to God's will.

Needs:

God never intended for the Christian life to be lived in isolation. Rather, He has provided the body of Christ as the natural source of Christian nurturing.

Adolescents especially need this support in order to maintain their self-control. Most adolescents are involved sexually because of personal intimacy needs, not just out of physical desire. Therefore, much of the work of enabling group members to avoid sexual immorality begins with providing them with loving, significant adults and supportive, concerned peers.

Goals:

The *leader's* goals include

(1) sensitizing group members to the important role they can play as "enablers;"

(2) guiding them toward a discovery of how they can specifically provide support for one another in the area of sexual decision-making;

(3) providing closure for this group so that members are prepared to continue in their maturity in Christ in regard to their sexual identity.

The *group members'* goals are

(1) to communicate with one another concerning practical ways to be supportive;

(2) to develop a personal support base for dealing with issues related to sexuality;

(3) to solidify commitments which may have resulted from this series.

Life Response:

Group members will conclude the series with a commitment to be one another's personal support base for positive peer influence.

Resource Materials:

___ copies of *Where Do You Think Sex Came From?*

___ Bibles

___ pens

HEARTBEAT
Lean on Me

"We All Need Somebody to Lean On" is a song that has been recorded by a number of singers, rearranged for all styles of music, and sung in many different types of settings. Perhaps this is because the words are so true. Everybody needs friends to go to for love, support, and acceptance no matter what happens.

☞ **Choose one or more of the following activities to lead the group members into an understanding of their roles as enablers of one another. All three activities have the interpersonal dynamics which illustrate the significance of peer support. You will want to use those which best fit the interests and size of your group.**

ACTIVITY ONE: TRUST FALL (7 + participants)

One member of the group will stand on a solid table or stage approximately 4–5 feet off the ground. This person will have his or her back to the rest of the group standing on the floor.

The group on the floor will face each other in two single-file lines. They will then extend their arms (you need at least three persons on each side), palms up, toward one another. Each person's hands should reach about halfway to the elbow of the person across from him. Their arms will form the "bed" onto which the person will fall backward.

Most likely, the catchers will want to join hands with the people across from them, but joined hands are actually far weaker because they break apart rather than flexing.

As long as the person standing falls back with a straight back and the group members are standing

shoulder to shoulder with their arms extended parallel to the floor, the group will have no trouble catching the person.

If you have never seen this activity done, you may want to practice with some friends beforehand or use a pad so that you are confident that what you are doing is completely safe.

Keep in mind that it is very unnatural to fall backward, and it takes an act of trust on the part of the group members for them to allow themselves to fall.

You may want to start by being the first to fall to set the example, or you may want to begin with someone who is very lightweight and build up to the largest.

ACTIVITY TWO: BODY PASS (7–9 participants)

Begin with all the group members in a circle, sitting upright on the floor with their legs extended so that their feet all meet in the center. You will need about 6–8 persons sitting in this circle.

Have one group member stand in the middle of all of the feet. This person is to stand stiff, crossing his or her arms in an "X" across his or her chest. (This is mandatory if there are any girls in the group. Otherwise they will be embarrassed and possibly physically hurt.)

The group members in the circle then hold out their arms to catch the person standing in the middle. When he or she is ready, the person in the middle falls in any direction—the falling person must remain stiff—and passed around the circle as fast as possible. Stop after about 10 passes, when the person gets dizzy, or the members' arms become tired—whichever comes first!

ACTIVITY THREE: TRUST WALK (2 + participants)

You will need a blindfold for every other person in the group. Each group member will get a partner, and each pair will be given a blindfold.

The group members will then blindfold their partners and take them on a 3–5 minute trust walk where the "sighted" persons will lead those "blind." After the time is up, they will reverse roles.

You can make the walk challenging by taking them outdoors or through an unfamiliar area.]

☞ [HINT: The learning which takes place in this type of discovery process results from the dynamics of group interaction. The learning comes to its full fruition in the "debriefing" which follows; be prepared to create an atmsophere of fun and cooperation without structured or forced thinking or analyzing during the activity.

Debriefing questions for these activities include:

● How did it feel to put your trust for your safety in someone else?

● How did it feel to be a part of the group being trusted by the person who was falling/walking?

● What does it take for you to be willing to trust someone?

● Who are the people in your life that you trust the most? How do they communicate to you that they can be trusted?

● Who is someone who trusts you? How have you showed that you are trustworthy?]

As we close this group study, we can continue to be key people in one another's lives by supporting each other in the commitments we have made. However, maintaining a relationship in which each of us is a person who can be trusted with others' thoughts and feelings requires consistency in our commitment to and communication with one another.

This final group time in the series will focus our efforts toward reaching that goal.

LIFELINE

Positive Peer Influence

In our last two group times, we looked at how we must take responsibility for ourselves in order to develop self-control and avoid giving into peer pressure. But what is our responsibility to one another?

As a group, let's look at two passages of Scripture and answer the following questions about each passage:

1. What are our responsibilities toward one another as Christians?

2. What are the reasons that God expects us to do this?

3. What benefits can we expect from taking responsibility to care for one another in these ways?

4. What are some practical ways in which we could apply these actions to supporting one another in our commitments to follow God's will sexually?

First, Hebrews 10:19-25, especially verses 24 and 25.

1.

2.

3.

4.

The second passage is 1 Thessalonians 5:12-24.

1.

2.

3.

4.

Many of us experience negative peer pressure to sensually express our sexuality. According to these verses, however, we are commanded to be a positive peer influence on one another. In other words, we are to encourage and support one another to do God's will. We are also commanded to confront our Christian friends if we see them headed for trouble. The confrontation is not, "Do what is right or I will not be your friend." (That's just another form of peer pressure.) Rather, the confrontation is, "I am your friend and I am concerned that what you are doing is hurting you and your relationship with God."

What qualities would you look for in a person that you would trust as one who could encourage, support, and confront you?

Powerful, Positive Peers

Below are three general categories in which we can be an encouragement and support to one another. They are also categories in which we should be confronted by our Christian friends if we are not seeking to serve God obediently.

    #1: Our Talk (Ephesians 5:1-4)

    #2: Our Actions Toward One Another (1 Corinthians 10:32; Colossians 3:16)

    #3: Our Lifestyle (1 Timothy 4:12)

 BODYLIFE

You: Positive Peer

In cell groups, let's list some of the ways we can be an encouragement to one another through our talk, actions, and lifestyle.

Life Responses

As a part of our growing in trust with one another, let's each choose one of the ways we just listed to provide support to the other members of the group. (You can use the following chart to keep a record of your base of support.)

Name _____ Means of Support _____
Name _____ Means of Support _____
Name _____ Means of Support _____
Name _____ Means of Support _____
Name _____ Means of Support _____
Name _____ Means of Support _____
Name _____ Means of Support _____

With the powerful love of your Father and the trustworthy support of your Christian friends, you can be successful in being the person God created you to be sexually!

Let's close this series in a prayer of thanksgiving for the gift of the person God has created each of us to be and for the provision and protection He provides for us.

☞ [HINT: Bringing this group to closure can include a number of other activities, depending on the level of commitment and relationship you have in your group. Some of those possibilities are listed below—but don't be afraid to create your own now that you are a veteran small group leader!

• Have each group member take a turn sitting in the middle of the group. With someone in the "hot seat," have the group members share points of affirmation about how that person has already been a source of encouragement through his or her talk, action, or example. It may be that the person has been honest about his or her own struggles or it could be that his or her strong commitment has challenged the rest of the group.

• Write out a corporate covenant which everyone can sign. This agreement could be a commitment to be there for one another in times of struggle as well as to be willing to confront one another if someone is slipping from his or her commitment.

• Pray as a group for each individual in the group, thanking God for each person and asking Him to strengthen each one as he or she seeks His will.

• Give an opportunity for group members to share commitments they have made in their LIFE RESPONSES and to be vulnerable in asking group members to hold them accountable for these commitments.]

☞ [HELP: Optional additional LIFE RESPONSES

1. Encourage group members to continue to pray for one another for specific commitments they have made.

2. Ask group members to share their commitments with another group of young people, perhaps even assist in leading this series with a small peer or younger group.

3. Follow up on group members' needs for more information by providing resources and programs on biblical sex education.

4. Organize a parent/teen series to cover some of these topics with parents. Or have a series for parents of pre-teens with the youth from this group participating in educating these parents on some of the issues and pressures facing adolescents in their sexual decision-making. The book *Youth Workers and Parents* by Karen Dockrey has a very fine chapter on sexuality plus an outline for leading a parent/teen meeting.

5. Commit to continue meeting with the group for another series in which the members can grow in their relationship with God and one another.]

Where Do You Think Sex Came From?

Please take a minute to fill out and mail this form giving us your candid reaction to this material. Thanks for your help!

In what setting did you use this Small Group Study? (Sunday School, youth group, midweek Bible study, etc.) _____

How many young people were in your group? _____

What was the age range of those in your group? _____

How long was your average meeting? _____

Do you plan to use other SonPower Small Group Studies? _____ Why or why not?

Did you and your young people enjoy this study? Why or why not?

What are the strengths and/or weaknesses of this leader's edition?

What are the strengths and/or weaknesses of the student book?

Would you like more information on SonPower Youth Sources?

Name	_____
Church name	_____
Church address	_____
	_____
Church phone	(_____)_____
Church size	_____

SGY04

SonPower Youth Sources Editor
Victor Books
1825 College Avenue
Wheaton, Illinois 60187